1° Tu

# DRUMS

MAKING ♪ MUSIC

KATE RIGGS

CREATIVE 🍎 EDUCATION

PUBLISHED *by* Creative Education
P.O. Box 227, Mankato, Minnesota 56002
*Creative Education is an imprint of The Creative Company*
www.thecreativecompany.us

DESIGN AND PRODUCTION *by* Ellen Huber
ART DIRECTION *by* Rita Marshall
PRINTED *in the* United States of America

PHOTOGRAPHS *by*
Dreamstime (William Davis, Lanaprima), Getty Images (Lars
Baron, C Squared Studios, Byron Cohen/NBC/NBCU Photo
Bank), iStockphoto (Maksym Bondarchuk, Ela Kwasniewski,
Juan Nel, peeterv), Shutterstock (ILYA AKINSHIN, amfroey,
Sergei Bachlakov, Vereshchagin Dmitry, Mike Flippo, Blaj
Gabriel, kajornyot, Ela Kwasniewski, Dragan Milovanovic,
mweichse, nvelichko, Dani Simmonds, Dmitry Skutin,
Polushkina Svetlana, TDC Photography, Pavel Vakhrushev,
Makarova Viktoria), Veer (Ocean Photography)

LIBRARY OF CONGRESS
CATALOGING-IN-PUBLICATION DATA
Riggs, Kate.
Drums / Kate Riggs.
p. cm. — (Making music)
SUMMARY: *A primary prelude to drums, including what*
*the percussion instruments look and sound like, basic instructions*
*on how to play them, and the kinds of music that feature them.*
Includes bibliographical references and index.

ISBN 978-1-60818-366-1
1. Drum—Juvenile literature. 1. Title.

ML1035.R54 2013
786.9—DC23    2013009493


9 8 7 6 5 4 3 2

# TABLE OF CONTENTS

# WHEN YOU HEAR A DRUM

Rumbling thunder. Waves crashing against rocks.

Horses' hooves pounding on the ground.

What do you think of when you hear a drum?

*A horse's hooves beat against the ground.*
*Ocean waves hit big rocks on shore.*

# THE PERCUSSION FAMILY

Musical instruments that sound and

look alike belong to a "family."

Drums are members of the percussion family.

Percussion instruments are

struck with a person's hands or with a stick.

*drumsticks*

Men in West Africa play
djembe (JEM-beh)
with their bare hands.

drumhead or skin

rim

frame

# PARTS OF A DRUM

| |
|---|
| The top of the drum is called the drumhead, or skin. |
| The rim holds the drumhead in place. |
| The drumhead is stretched over the frame of the drum. |
| When you hit the drumhead, it **vibrates**. |
| This makes the air inside the frame vibrate, too. |

*Ropes, twisted pieces of animal hide, and other materials can serve as rims.*

# DRUM SHAPES AND MATERIALS

Many drums look like round boxes.

Some are shaped like bowls.

Some drums have **tuning** screws on the rim.

The bottom of the drum is called the base.

Many drums are made out of wood or metal.

Some drums are made all of steel.

*tuning screw*

*djembe*

*snare drum*

*bongos*

*timpani*

*steel drum*

# KINDS OF DRUMS

Big drums make deeper and louder

sounds than small drums.

Timpani are some of the biggest drums.

You use a stick called a beater

or mallet to strike the timpani.

A tambourine (*tam-bur-EEN*) is a very small drum.

It has loose metal disks that jingle.

*tambourine*

Timpani are also called kettledrums. They are shaped like big pots, or kettles.

# PLAYING THE DRUMS

Drummers can stand or sit to play drums.

You hold the sticks in both hands.

Or you rest the palm of your hand on the drumhead.

Then you tap the drumhead to keep the beat.

*It is easier to stand up to play taller drums.*
*Others can be played while sitting down.*

# EARLY DRUMS

Drums are some of the oldest

instruments in the world.

People in Africa and China played

drums thousands of years ago!

Many drums have not changed much over time.

*African drum*

Large drums were used in Chinese cities to let people know what time it was.

*Orchestra drummers watch the conductor to know when to hit which drum.*

# DRUM MUSIC

Drummers in an orchestra (*OR-keh-struh*)

stand behind a lot of drums.

A drummer in a rock band sits to play a drum kit.

Snare, tom-tom, and bass drums are the types of

drums in a drum kit. Other percussion instruments

called cymbals are also in a drum kit.

ride cymbal

hanging tom-toms

crash cymbal

hi-hat

snare drum

floor tom-tom

bass drum

# A DRUMMER PLAYS

A drummer sits at his drum kit.

The stage lights up.

He taps his sticks together in the air four times.

Then he plays a booming note.

People in the crowd scream as the drums keep the beat!

Abe Cunningham has played with a band called Deftones since 1988.

# MEET A DRUMMER

*Evelyn Glennie was born in 1965 in Scotland.*

*She began to lose her hearing when she was eight.*

*She has been **deaf** since she was 12. Evelyn plays drums*

*and other percussion instruments all over the world.*

*She **tours** a lot in the United States and other countries.*

*She does not like wearing shoes when she plays.*

*She can feel the music better with her bare feet!*

*Evelyn Glennie played at the opening ceremony of the 2012 Olympic Games.*

## GLOSSARY

**deaf**: *unable to hear*

**tours**: *travels to different cities within a country or around the world to do concerts*

**tuning**: *fixing the pitch, or sound, of an instrument*

**vibrates**: *shakes or moves up and down rapidly*

## READ MORE

Ganeri, Anita. *Drums and Percussion Instruments.* North Mankato, Minn.: Smart Apple Media, 2012.

Levine, Robert. *The Story of the Orchestra.* New York: Black Dog & Leventhal, 2001.

Storey, Rita. *The Drum and Other Percussion Instruments.* North Mankato, Minn.: Smart Apple Media, 2010.

## WEBSITES

**Drums and Percussion**
www.rhythmweb.com/kids/index.html
*Watch and listen to kids using different kinds of drums around the world.*

**Super Sounding Drums**
http://pbskids.org/zoom/activities/sci/
supersoundingdrums.html
*Make drums out of things in your home. Find out which drums are the loudest!*

*Every effort has been made to ensure that these sites are suitable for children, that they have educational value, and that they contain no inappropriate material. However, because of the nature of the Internet, it is impossible to guarantee that these sites will remain active indefinitely or that their contents will not be altered.*

## INDEX